This book belongs to

HappyFeet

One of the **HappyFeet** Kids

ISBN 13: 978-0-9992492-6-0 (Paperback)
ISBN 13: 978-0-9992492-8-4 (Hardcover)
ISBN 13: 978-0-9992492-7-7 (eBook)

Illustrations and cover design © 2018 by Eminence System
Editing by Donna Dione

Printed and bound in the United States of America.

First Printing 2018

Published by HappyFeet Books
146 Essex Street
Deep River, CT 06417

www.HappyFeetBooks.com

The HappyFeet Kids
Search For Treasure
GOLDEN GOAL
WRITTEN BY
DONALD DIONE
ILLUSTRATIONS BY
EMINENCE SYSTEM

Meet the HAPPYFEET KiDS

Ahoy Matey! I'm Captain Coach Jan. This here is my crew - **The HappyFeet Kids**. Come sail with us if you want to find treasure too.

Hi there, I'm Chen. I love searching for buried treasure.

This is Bob the Bobcat.
He is a baby bobcat that swallowed a magic soccer ball.
He helps the kids on their adventures, and the kids use their soccer skills to help Bob.

Hi, I'm José, and I like pirate costumes.

Hello, my name is Holly. I like that pirates sail on big ships.

I'm Ricky, and I love to go on pirate adventures.

Hi, my name is Zara. I like to look for mermaids when I'm being a pirate.

I'm Sara, and I like pretending to be a pirate because I like the sea.

Coach Jan asked, "Who likes treasure?"

The kids shouted, "I do!"

Coach Jan asked, "Who likes pirates?"

Again, the kids shouted, "I do!"

Coach Jan then asked, "What do pirates go on?"

Chen answered, “Pirate ships.”

Finally, Coach Jan asked, “Who wants to go with me on the pirate ship and search for the buried treasure?”

The HappyFeet Kids jumped with joy, yelling, “I want to look for treasure!!”

After dressing like pirates, the HappyFeet Kids climbed aboard the pirate ship, where they found Captain Coach Jan waiting for them.

Captain Coach Jan asked, "Do you have your sea legs crew?"

"Aye aye, Captain," answered the crew.

Then they saw Bobs' sleeping bag and ran over to see if they wanted join the crew.

"Ahoy Matey!!" shouted Ricky when he found the Bobs were still asleep.

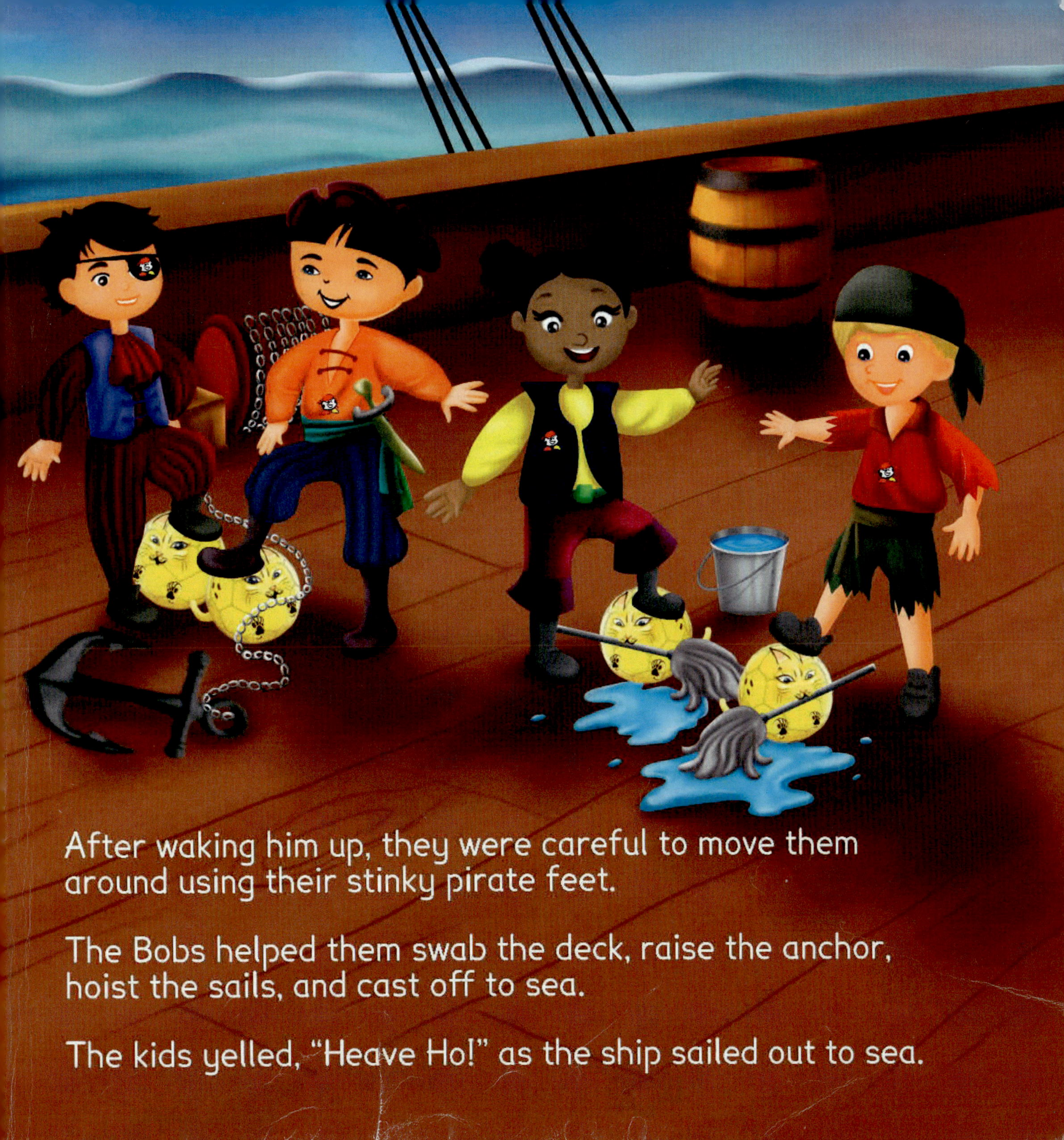

After waking him up, they were careful to move them around using their stinky pirate feet.

The Bobs helped them swab the deck, raise the anchor, hoist the sails, and cast off to sea.

The kids yelled, "Heave Ho!" as the ship sailed out to sea.

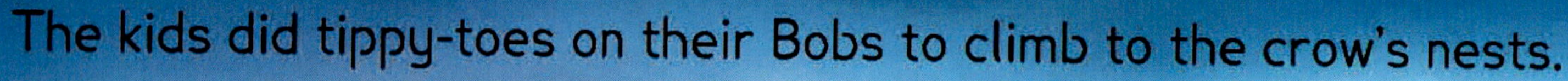

The kids did tippy-toes on their Bobs to climb to the crow's nests.

They peered through their telescopes towards the ocean.

José saw some sharks circling the ship.

Sara watched dolphins leap from the sea.

Holly saw mermaids on the far away rocks.

Ricky noticed the flying fish sailing above the waves.

Zara said, "Thar she blows!" as a whale swam past the ship.

Chen looked around until he saw --- **PIRATES!!!**

Quickly, the kids climbed down to the deck, where the Bobs helped them load the cannons.
Boom! Boom!! BOOM!!!
The cannons roared as the kids and the Bobs fired them.

The other pirates sailed off, not wanting to battle with the legendary "**Golden Goal**."

After sailing far into the sea, the kids found an island and rowed ashore.

The kids said, "Help me find the treasure Bob," and started dribbling Bob around in search of the buried treasure.

They found an "X" in the sand and knew it marked the spot.

By doing tick-tocks, with Bob holding a shovel in his mouth, the kids were able to dig up the treasure chests.

In order to open the locked chests, the kids had to do a scissors move with the Bobs to find the magic keys.

"Tap your foot next to Bob, that foot slides in front of Bob, your other foot slides behind Bob," called Captain Coach Jan.

“Get away from me Bob,” said the kids as they kicked Bob away with the outside of their feet.

Magically, the keys appeared as the Bobs rolled away.

“Argh,” cheered Sara and Zara as they picked up their keys.

Unlocking the chest, the kids found all sorts of treasure.

Holly shouted, "Look at all of this booty."

They found gold, silver, rings, necklaces, and jewels.

They were so excited that they asked Captain Coach Jan if they could sing a song to celebrate.

"Why shiver me timbers," answered Captain Coach Jan as she started to sing.

"Roll, roll, roll your Bob, gently through the sea.

Merrily, merrily, merrily, merrily, soccer is so fun!"

The kids sang too, as they followed Captain Coach Jan back to the row boats .

As they sang the song again, the kids changed the words,

"Roll, roll, roll your Bob, gently through the sea.

Kick your Bob at your coach and listen to her squeal."

The kids started kicking their Bobs at Captain Coach Jan as she ran away.

Every time she was hit by a Bob, she gave a little yelp and cried, "MUTANY!"

Finally, she reached the row boats and went back to the ship.

The kids gathered their Bobs and followed.

GOLDEN GOAL

Captain Coach Jan said, "Mutinous crew, it is now time to walk the plank."
They all lined up and walked to the end of the plank.
Then, they each jumped over Bob, and ...

Instead of landing in the water with the sharks, the kids amazingly ended up back in their secret hideout.

Coach Jan pulled out her **Magic Stamp**.

Each kid became strong and fast as she put a stamp on the back of their hand.

After such a wonderful day of treasure hunting, the kids all went home.

But not before yelling – **ARGH!!! WE LOVE HAPPYFEET!!!**

About HappyFeet Programs and Books

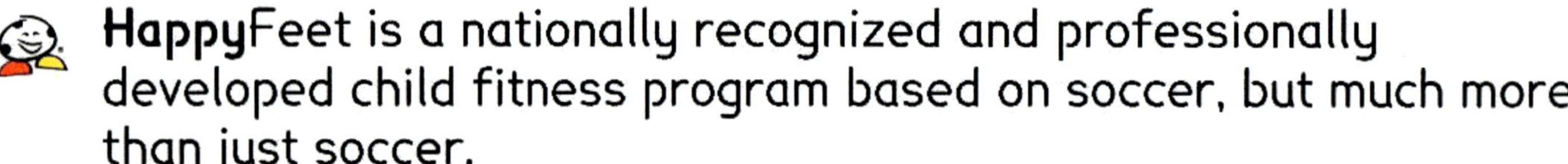

- **Happy**Feet is a nationally recognized and professionally developed child fitness program based on soccer, but much more than just soccer.

- **Happy**Feet's creative and innovative "**STORY TIME WITH A SOCCER BALL**" methodology enables children to enhance their cognitive growth, improve their balance and coordination, develop their self-confidence, and have a **BLAST** doing it!!!

- **Happy**Feet introduces children to the wonderful world of soccer, through the use of exciting, imaginary adventures with the **Happy**Feet soccer ball - **Bob the Bobcat**.

- **Happy**Feet books bring these adventures home. When parents read The **Happy**Feet Kids books to their children, the educational benefits of **Happy**Feet programming grows exponentially as fitness is combined with literacy!

- **Happy**Feet programs and **Happy**Feet books help children develop core academic skills and physical fitness in a proven, age-appropriate, and fun manner.

- Visit www.HappyFeetBooks.com to learn more.

- Visit www.HappyFeetBooks.com/locations to learn about **Happy**Feet programs near you.

THE HAPPYFEET KIDS

CREATING BRAVE, CREATIVE LEADERS, ONE STORY AT A TIME!!

*The **Happy**Feet Kids* books are based on proven **Happy**Feet class adventures, so we know kids will love them. We believe they also give parents a deeper understanding of **Happy**Feet programming. The mission of **Happy**Feet is to help children grow into brave, creative leaders for life. Our books and classes enable children to expand their imaginations and grow their motor skills in a supportive environment. The lessons learned from **Happy**Feet are retained for the rest of their lives.

On the last page of every book, you will find **Happy**Feet Soccer moves for beginner, intermediate, and advanced children. Please give them a try, and you will be combining literacy and fitness in the true **Happy**Feet spirit and developing the next brave, creative leader as a **Happy**Feet Kid!

Thank you for allowing us to help your child on this journey!!!

HAPPYFEET SOCCER SKILLS

Beginner

Ball Rolls

Bob under heal – Bob mid-foot – Bob under toe – Bob mid-foot – Bob under heal

Intermediate

Walking Ball Roll

Roll Bob with right foot's sole, then left foot's sole, then right foot's sole

Advanced

Scissors

Tap left foot - left foot in front of Bob - Bob in the middle
right foot behind Bob - kick Bob away with outside of right foot

Made in the USA
Columbia, SC
17 December 2018